GROWLERY

Katherine Horrex lives in Manchester.
Growlery is her first collection.

KATHERINE HORREX

Growlery

CARCANET

First published in Great Britain in 2020 by
Carcanet
Alliance House, 30 Cross Street
Manchester M2 7AQ
www.carcanet.co.uk

A CIP catalogue record for this book is
available from the British Library.

ISBN 978 1 78410 989 9

Book design by Andrew Latimer
Printed in Great Britain by SRP Ltd, Exeter, Devon

The publisher acknowledges financial
assistance from Arts Council England.

CONTENTS

For my family

GROWLERY

MAINFRAME

Light the colour of deep-sea fish
tacks down fibre optics.

    If you could peer down the lines
and see through the neon
you'd discover molecular numbers.

In cladded glass tubes, where numbers
       swarm and are desperate to pixelate,
I'm only a blanched thing searching.

At the line's other end,
      your face a satellite dish.

FOUR MUSES

What to say to my muse the power plant
who makes auras for the city's night hours
with a sputter of wattage and volts?

What to say to my muse the steelworks
who sends hot blasts down the standpipe
for fig trees to thrive in?

What to say of the pigments
rolled out in testing chambers
by my latest muse the chemical plant?

What to say when the power plant
hums and clicks and shines
like a fairylit woodwind instrument?

What to say when the belting out
of playground pieces gives way
to the making of girders for steelworks?

What to say when McBrides carpets the Roch
and makes soft, six foot dams
out of flammable detergent?

How to contain them all,
do justice to their invention of
and disregard for protocol,

how to juggle their sweltering egos
when I walk where figs
leave oily splats on the towpath,

street lamps turn pale in daylight
and latex dries in a bucket slung round
a rubber plant's tapped green trunk?

GOAT FELL

Only after living in its shadow for a month
can I say that its attraction has worn off,
that I went there once or twice
seeking a river locals mentioned
not long after I arrived,

nose raw with the churchy strangeness
of water underfoot and the valley
closing over like a hand. My boots
were sucked by moss and a slip in the mud
nearly had me kneeling

as if I were a pilgrim at the island's altar.
More like it was the butcher's block
in the craggiest backstory of this particular ayr
and what I'd heard before meant that halfway up,
when the wind ran round a slate grey howff,

it seemed to whisper 'Rose, Rose'. The way a boiler
in an old, old house takes on the voice
of someone who's not there. Now I do not want to go
into that cold mountain dream with feet scrying
for the summit in the screes and murder in the fellside's bones.

BREXIT

The city has been stamped with leaves
and is a mail bag, waiting to be posted somewhere.
Houses, on a hillside, stacked like letters
spilling over so the wind can almost snatch them.

Its streets are grit filled markings on a shoe sole
cambering uneasily at the heel
and worn into themselves like grafted skin.
The tarmac has a greasy sheen.

Only people's backs, hunched towards shopping,
confirm life happens here, wrapped in cagoules.
People personable as tents zipped shut,
canvas for the rain to write on.

They lean into windows lit like oilseed,
believe they're holding something by its horns.
Their houses ache like letters that leave something bad
unsaid. But the whole world knows their thoughts.

Theirs was only the stale and temporary discretion
of booths at a polling station.
Houses on a hillside turn to banners
filling with the wind, which never takes them far.

LANDGRAB

Lumps from different quarries
slake down together.

Hands in the sediment,
each kernel and nub

shoulders through slip
when I pour it.

Earth's fingerprints over mine.
A googolplexus of recorded lives.

PARLIAMENT, FALLEN

We can afford to know nothing
beyond concrete, the concatenate
glower of windows.
The street below is a shortcut
for us, though we hate to be dripped on
by clothes horse balconies.

Looking up means a view
through a dark kaleidoscope,
where leaden basslines beat
at the air with all the thunder of hives.
It calls to mind the shuttered
instability of hearts.

As a disused mall this polygon
could be acceptable. Instead
we wonder if there are people
in the hidden parts of the panopticon,
waiting to reveal just how
brittle they've become,

a helter-skelter's skeleton
bleach-stripped by the sun,
the sweet vomit smell of bleach itself,
and we consider
whether something built purely to function
can only fall to ruin,

the city's sirens congregating
in these quads,
where anyone talking talks boldly
in a voice that spreads to fill the space
shaped to keep its own
community of echoes.

HOUSE OF OTHER TONGUES

Day & night the garrulous stairwell
tattles of each departure and arrival

walls so thin
talk in the house
floats through them
& clucks opinion on
the manner in which you draw your curtains shut.

Day & night in the big kitchens
dishwater falls from raddled sponges;
one thick, greasy drip
each time you wring.

In the lobby
parental letters sit & advise
against other-than-English-abroad
& there are adverts offering meetings with someone
who can help with 'accent reduction'.

A poor voice
ne'er carries.

Day & night regional accents
are disapproved of the world over
by those who want tongues smooth as glass slippers,
to sound unaffected by whereabouts,
for some reason
better able to broadcast
something equated with knowledge.

Day & night this *is* the house
of other tongues,
whole salted fishhead with ice in the gills,

dried crayfish
twirling under tapwater
like sycamore seed in the sink,
the bang of utensils
a strange glossolalia

when day & night the fridges are loaded
with sweating tupperware
by those whose tongues stay
locked in the mouth's hermitage
light years off from conversation

til they start with laughter
& words they didn't know they know

AUTONOMOUS LANDFILL

When I come back I'll be a refuse tip,
twenty containers
on a tarmacked hilltop,

I'll spill along your road
and cover it with the foil corners
of trays from the hotdog stand,

leave a tonne of matter:
pulped bones jawed by lorries
til you're hidden by the foetor

of everything melting at once.
I'll drop an abattoir on the school
where the world seemed far and immense.

You'll be as consequential as an index
in a catalogue of disused sat navs.
Your spine crenelated with Perspex.

Fragments in your back when I bury the shoreline
with a torrent of sliced up LCDs
and rust from a ditched bi-plane.

Bosch vacuums, Hieronymus
Hellscapes, a jar of pickled lymph nodes
crammed down your hometown's chimneys

the desktop motherboard still storing
that jpeg you sent of a topless woman posed
as the queen – hand up skirt – underscoring

this & all the rest, which includes
the stuff I'm too kind to mention,
turf I'll caramelise in the memorial gardens
                    next to an old tramp obsessed with nudes.

Your windows, your doorjambs,
every exit of your home, to mock you,
I'll seal with DNA from a trillion unaberrated genomes.

AFRAID IS A TOWN

Where mills made of lead
snuff your phone signal out as fast
as an all-seeing foreman,

where midnight footfall
three houses down
sounds like intruders in your home,

where the shadowy clatter of hooves
threatens to lend more furlongs to the dark,
but is just a paint tin rolling in the street,

where the scene of Lowry's 'The Chapel'
looks even more 'down at heel'
now weed-clogged, cracked and chapel-less,

where, on a hill, a church bell
hungers, behind wooden slats, for every hour
to shake off festering bats,

where, although no-one's there, you feel
fists, or knives, waiting to meet you in anger,
throbbing in pockets of air,

where people still say the rain
carries radioactive traces,
landing on your head even as you watch

a hundred paper lanterns descend
delicately round a kink in the cloud
over a monument that honours the dead.

BOTTLE KILNS

when they smashed the brick their eyes
turned hot as grains in a sand storm.
Men who went out into smoke covering the streets,

all doors dark, and even the snow
as it fell. Men with blank stomachs ministering
to coal's snap, crackle and pop.

Three storeys of buckling firebricks held
with thin iron hoops.
Men on their way to pile the saggars,

bearing them on their heads as they went
like women walking ten miles to a well.
Men who heated the stacked saggars

and plied the pottery with 15 tonnes
of burning coal, who lined their bellies with spirits
so they could reckon with the firemouth,

wet rags to their faces
running in and out to press themselves
with the heat. Men who made sure

40, 000 bone china plates
were vitrified and cooling in the warehouse.
Who pocketed, from bosses, shilling pieces, silicosis.

BUTTERMERE

When the lake came for us
a dark hue zipped across it
like a tent's outer shell being shut.
It stung us as it rose
from out of the stillness
drawing the surface over us.

I swam in it that afternoon
which was warm and perfectly current-less
but for the wind, rushing to knock me,
bidding that I pray

to the pebbles,
the shale and broken bottles,
a trip-me-up dirty old rope
mooring the shadows
for god knows how long.

Feet off the grit floor it was fine.
The lake stirred in fits
but was no real threat to movement further out,

the body a bow that way,
rolling through the water's cool slaps,
delving for the other side.

But, out there alone,
and not a quarter of the way across,
I found I had to turn

for fear I'd meet the pucker
of miles-dark depths
and things touched fearlessly
by water only.

I wanted no part in that journey.

PAREIDOLIA

Melted likeness
in the mountain's
landslide

like the prophet
in a crust of bread,
defers to the face

in the brain
that is part idolatry,
part will to survive.

We use it to find
our parents first,

the food that is rooted
in gazes returned.

Then come the faces in faces
imposed by loneliness,
an old friend found
in a stranger's nod

providing a foothold
in foreignness

Is there a lowness
to this clinging?

No fresh greeting is uttered.

These faces are the grasses
that weave underfoot,
slicked down by forward motion.

OMEN

Seven corpse flowers have bloomed in America,
ugly as drunks with their tongues out
reeking of puke on subway benches.

Pancetta soaked in cleaning agent.
Huge flies grub all over the spathes,
formidable as black ops.

Crowds gather in greenhouses to watch
the spadixes rise like synchronised swimmers
out of each monumental petal head,

camping out until the plant
becomes a strange, depleted candle, its rubbery wick
a bouncy castle cut off from the pump.

Clock hands snip away and the sun folds
under the horizon, leaving stars
piled above the arum's hidden corm.

On a podium elsewhere, several figures
stand to dance around their politics, bowing out
of the Q & A before the hustings.

IRON TREES

Tree parts were gathered by the dozen
from vendors in Jingdezhen,

long staffs chewed by the delicate lanterns,
by wood ears puffed up with poisons.

Trunks with chatter marks from fungi,
ashen nebs the shape of Shanghai,

maps of the studio's neighbourhood,
criss-crossing into the roughwood.

Shields wrought with pulp and wasps' nests
emerged from the foundry casts

to be bolted at quizzical angles,
quaint as a lamplit shambles

until the ferrites did their work
of weaving through the bark.

Rust, the trees' deepening autumn,
coats each reaching limb with red, red lichen

and lava coloured sap sets in
to the notches, the striation.

Night looks down at our undead trees,
the governments propped up with dynasties!

That owl must have called
as many times as there are rings
in the tree it lives in,
a ranging enquiry
of Who Who Who
skimmed into the night
        with a stammer of branch bark.

He shears the air as he hunts, his frosty,
cobwebbed, kudzu-covered owlets
rasping in the nest of his heart
where they cough up gibletty pellets

of Who, and
           Who, and
Who?

What aviary
my life must seem to him...
even after his day crossing some mote ridden barn
where he waited for soft things
to scurry.

It's not long
since I read
that *plants are able*
to drain the energy of other plants
nearby. The owl
swoops to land,

no louder than hay stalks
falling in long grass.

SEVEN FLOODED VILLAGES

Time as puddles filtering back to air,
rope   lanterns in the square are strung along.
Newspaper gone crisp - balled up from the edges inward, an update pushed
downscreen   by updates.
Time as an interactive map,   the space between Now and Pangea
                                                welling with land.

A coffee warehouse camped in, restored to industry.
Time as sand   flushed to surface
then resettled,   Xe Pian and Mekong rerouted, disturbed.
Water mark a rising gap below roof tiles,   houses
shrunk to apexes,   brick islands.
A mountain's worth of water and then a mountain range's
worth. Old bombs buried under floods
in burrows. Time as lost as a lizard's tail
soon as the stone   makes contact

GREY NATURAL LIGHT

It breaks through voile and stains
like tannin leaching into a cup;

(The voile bunches like tissue paper
strewn by an elephant).

Carbon filters into rooms
invisibly, on the back of the world's breath.

Dioxide. It is not unexpected.
Nor is it hindered; almost every car

trails ashes down the roads' long
crawl of grau, grau, grau. Not much

today it seems will grow but we may dig
for graphite, paint elephants in the sky azure.

POTTER'S WHEEL SONG

What skeletons we dine with
when we bring our mouths
to the quarry each mealtime!

I drub them with the wooden rib,
spin them into tableware,

make of them plates to be bisqued,
committed to stone.

They'll cousin statues
in that drum-shaped firebox, the kiln.

LIGHTLORN

Flowers in the branches stubbed out
by terrace brows. Sunlight
down the road at narrow intervals.
Wet grasses pricking our ankles.
The gate in need of lifting to its latch.
Our lurcher greets us, sniffs round the yard
to check it's not been moved.
We stock the fridge, leave windows
half-open so days end with the chitter
of starlings, sucked back into eaves
like smoke inhaled by a chimney
in a home movie on rewind.

DOORWAY

imprints of tongues in ice:
Flemish glass in the front door
of nan and grandad's house blurring
our sense of the hallway,
where pink or blue
floated up from our Disney vision
of days begun in the kitchen:
toast etched free of its whiskery burn,
every seven o'clock observed.
Pink sweater full of biscuits.
Blue sweater infused with imperial leather.
One day I heard about the near
heartbreak of their move into separate
houses, where they for a while reclaimed
protestant and catholic differences,
that, or they sat staring into new circumstance,
their cold milk mulled
with floating, twice used teabags
until one of them picked up the phone
and cajoled the other with admissions
of stupidity. Twenty years since
and it's unlikely whoever lives here
collects Toby jugs or frowns
at the crossword with a work-desk
bank pen tucked behind an ear,
or keeps a space for special occasions
so that it smells of powdery
showroom upholstery.
Not wishing to knock or discover
eerie similarity, I go, before my tongue
fixes on glass

if I lived here, and cultivated a certain kind of pride,
I'd wish the world would visit and not make these kinds of observations,
would see instead colourful monorail cars (devoid of emptiness)
wide, bright cinemas on wide, clean streets.

High-rises built from caddy grilles.
Grass roots hope throughout the conurbations.
Not this spreading aftershock of disassembly
now capital has moved to evolve more cheaply,
leaving burnt-out multi-storeys as its ammonites.

Nor press conference after press conference after press conference about
how to fix the fuse of shorted neighbourhoods.
How the best corners are forever halogen lit
(but home to children who swear
    they hear wifi chirping to the point of distraction).

How there are two kinds of living:
if yours ain't the best, you get drunk & aimless on a bmx,
patted down by cops.

The blighted clapboard peels and curls like birch rot –
it being too easy / sensationalist to say *flame*.
Drama can lead to a broken fascia
& there are plenty of those
in this birthplace of the junkie
singing, 'grease my palm with silver',
this pioneerdom of going under
in the age of fibre optics,
casinos in the only quarter glowing,
townhouses put to pasture,
& the Ford plant's bitten windows whistling…

I'd hope no one would mention any of that.
Or talk about mortgages flooding
people out of their homes
to a river where ice floats with jellyfish passivity.

The slightest breeze
can shake a broken fascia.

Blight so strong it has its own map.
Whole districts, from which humanity
has been redacted.

THE GENTRIFIED WATER

While the swamp that eats Jakarta
                    eats Jakarta
a man sells drinking straws he's pulled from mud.
For poverty makes us drink from our foundations
                    til they crumble into the cisterns.

For into the gaps
Jakarta falls as if staved in
by its own glass towers,
      its unfathomably constructed hotels filled

with engineers who cite blueprints
and want to tack their dams across the sea,
which will still enact the opposite of 'polder'.

For already our streets fall over each over
like the keys of a neglected piano

trash spilling from the shacks
so that each one resembles a weir.

For we exist in a capital of geobrinkmanship
leaving in hope that our home
will drop into its own cracks quietly
and then be reconstructed
somewhere on the other side,

making wells of our bellies
to transfer to the city
not yet Jakarta

for if we do not leave, we live
as fodder for the flood.
What can we do
but call to the hotels
we sink beneath?

CLEVER PUPPETEERS

Money forms in clouds far from the metropolising cities.
As soon as it lands words rise
re. who should drink it – for how much,
aldermen flocking to barter in favour of their parishes,
minute ledgers filled:

the yolking of nature should spread from cattle to land
but most of it runs elsewhere!

A thousand rash phrases
about a deep & placid seal
between two moors.

Under the lake two glib settlements
have turned to aqueous rubble,
enough of it to somehow weight a city down,

& in spite of ancient farmers' plans
to clot them with manure,
the lake's long pipes instigate
                another skyscraper

another precinct fed by moors strapped
to the city filled with water the colour of ink
from sixteen million bills.

Money forms in clouds far from the metropolising cities.
As soon as it lands, towers rise

LOOKING AT THE SCULPTURES

At the city's end, three crane claws
have snagged on the coast, where they hang

question mark style and anchorish, 'like badly
placed moorings', says one Tripadvisor

review. Friends of the sculptor
tell how no one wanted them in Donostia;

cafes preferred along the promenade.
Not workings from the shipyard.

For some, smiles Chillida, my reliquaries
are shorthand for bad trade, crippled euros.

Who cares that they reach for one another
from their coastal plinths, and, unable to meet

resort to the stance of sailors, clenching
biceps to confirm their worth?

The bay spreads over the low wall
and a girl takes a picture with a go pro.

Someone walks past, unhooking the top
from a bottle. Who knows what rankles

these loose knots into rearing from the surf,
like confused unspooling octopuses?

LAPWINGS IN FALLOWFIELD

They sit with the road's oily
tang in their nares,
their bodies like helmets in grass.

Younger ones look like soil
on snow and nest
in the adults' thick feathers.

My sister and I at somebody's
wedding, when we hid
under somebody's dress.

INNER CITY SUBURB

we can enter a property by force
even when that property
is not the property intended

thus the word must be ramshackle –
thousands of buses jolting
a high street skewiff
    peppery gusts from the designated lanes –
rife enough to lift pavements

a big spree of archways
with fuel-blackened date stones
    above shops working a turnover
which fractures off-kilter doors

interchangeable to the point that
3 policemen tried to launch a sting on my old flat,
instead of the café named in their warrant
the week the M.E.N. reported
three nearby rapes that started
with men waving fake ID

the church a yoga studio at night
incense rising from its pulpit
    next door to that place
every meal rolled out of
wrapped in a bank statement's
minus numbers

flyers gummed to shoes
in walkways under the halfbuilds,
the many future chances
            to flesh out my old life's ghost

which paces every first floor
of the main road's shop front row
along the roulette wheel
of <to let> or <for sale>

past clusters of potential investors
wooed with tours
of bedroom vistas,

and landlords
repainting kitchenettes

EYEPIECE

This stone's afraid to hold the secrets it contained.
Waits for the sea to bore its holes.
Water billows back,
an exploding refuse bag
with a strength that turns the stone to sand.
A piece of carpet for a pipit.

This matters little.
The stone does not want to launch
another ammonite discovery.
It seeks no permanence and currently
enjoys life as a drain.
It will be just as comfortable
bearing the weight of the sea.

UNDERTOW

Roofs round the square
crest against the sky. The churches,
with their flags, turn naval in a blink.

As worms are teased to the grass by gulls
so the loud sun has drawn us to unload
our buckets of talk in town,

which would be a beach if it weren't
for the buses, their flurries
of hot alloy breath.

How like wishes to reveal
themselves, even when they're buried –
the way ripples on an ocean wheel like fins.

WOOD FROG

There's tedium in the veins
of the roses you gave me.
Their heads hang stiffly
over dried out stalks.
I forgot to water them, or rather
thought I'd watered them but hadn't.

Now that I have means nothing,
though the stems puff and the heads
begin to lift, trembling as ice
trembles in the early yards of spring.
Though the buds begin to chafe
with light and grow

the way a wood frog sparks
itself to life after a full winter
cased in tundra, its solid black
nut of a body soft again,
eyes lifting from the thaw
of its torso in answer to the storm

in its cells. No such urgency
is found in a vase, though there may
have been a hope in giving,
in the short brightening of this room
where a corolla frowningly describes
a person's heart.

POLYCYSTIC

Ultrasound shows them:
moth holes
in the vacuum of the ovum.

Medics refer to 'strings of pearls,'
some of which teethe,
their tissue is that much an assortment of cells,

casting out hair and bone to become
small sacks of offerings stored in the tract.

Even without the scan wand
painting this wall before children,
they are clear
and ground me like pebbles.

I resolve to leave the hospital for home
where I don't keep
plants in urns, their roots all stoppered
with gravel.

I'll try to induce myself,
conducting the passage of a lunar month
through measures of darkness and light.

I'm waiting for my body to snow.

SMALL BATCH

Some Goldman Sachs financier ordered plates
to be made and sent to her in Brooklyn. They were
cooking in the kiln and would've been glowing

when I went towards the cellar
the solstice I miscounted the steps, misfooted the dark
and failed to grip the hand rail as I fell.

Some of the bones in my foot turned tectonic
when I tried to stall the impact.
An ankle rotated and split.

Concrete chill oozed through my winter
coat. I screamed into the night.

My partner yelled, the way some bankers do, looking up
at screens when the FTSE crashes.

On the ground,
I stayed, hand shoved under my coat and jumper,
   til I felt a movement – a flutter – that was not, thank god,
the moon dissolving.

STARLINGS / SLOW SHUTTER SPEED

barnacled maps of the roost to be joined
come winter   printed in negative

CHIMNEY

calm smoke
rises vertically...

vertically rises:
calm smoke.

Vertically calm,
smoke rises.

Calm smoke,
Smoke calm

Smoke rises,
vertically calm.

Vertically, smoke
calm-rises.

Smoke-smoke,
calm-calm.

Rises vertically,
calm smoke

WAKING IN TWOS

A clock knocks time
between four walls
where we lie caught up
in the excellent rejection
of all company but each others',
immune to the pendulum
as if it were the call
of animals elsewhere –
cockerels crowing about
unfinished revolution,
so that whoever still sleeps, or slept,
is on infinite alert, half consciously. Not us.
Next door's farm winds down,
its owner dead by his own gun
for some days now. Not us
and lorries light our room with commerce.

WHAT FARM IS THIS?

In their trees afterdark birds hush
        the hollering I've grown to love
though it echoes round the edges
        of my almost-sleep. The railing
of gulls starts & I set out to mix silage
        to throw to the pigs, slow sun
rising with the ease of a provincial town
waking to work,

& the light is different here I'm sure, roaring through
the atmosphere over these less-loved regions
linked to cities only by B-roads and trains
cutting across with hauls of people
who don't know this place
to disapprove

though I hear them
hissing at our quiet ownership
of lives & land,

days cows leave off their lowing
as soon as the machines
have loosed them from a hefty milking
& stand, as the folksy saying claims,
because of rain.

I scarcely need drive them over the fields,
into their slow-eyed standing.

I hear this sky,
the birds ignite it in brisk clouds.

THE FARM OF A THOUSAND CROPS

in furrows' clenched ears
a sea of forks prepares to sway.

Every seed a shell
in which a future's curled.

Leaves in each valve,
fair as new thatch.

My nipples prickle
with milk itch.

OUT OF PLACE

Street lamp high
and staring from the leafy
rough-edged sea,

a rose bloom
halfway up the tall
conifer hedge.

I was fifteen
and in this room
almost half my life ago

when a great aunt mocked
my bee-sting breasts.
They were under a tie-dye shirt.

Seeing the flower,
its thorns hidden
like the plugs and wires

of a string of fairy lights,
I remember something else –
how a mangy stalactitic tooth

was found growing
from the centre
of her concave cheek.

MOON JAR AND MOONDARK

I wouldn't think to hide in such a lampish vessel
as the moon jar, its hemispheres of bright clay joined
for the storage of rice, soy sauce and alcohol.
Porcelain is not especially given to the clandestine,
though here it calls something to my mind
of the old noun for a wife's nest egg,
hidden from her husband.

'Bottle Kilns' was written after I visited the Gladstone pottery in Stoke-on-Trent and read about the action male potteries staff took to ensure that women were unable to work as throwers, or to load the kilns, upon their introduction to the workplace.

The 'Brexit' described was imagined after I saw a news clip showing a woman in Hull saying she voted leave 'because I'm sick of seeing Polish families on my street'.

'Clever Puppeteers' was written about Thirlmere in Cumbria. Upon the commissioning of Thirlmere into a reservoir, John Ruskin said of Manchester that it 'should be put to the bottom of Thirlmere,' and of people in Manchester, 'that there is no profit in the continuance of their lives.' This interested me because, were he to post this on Twitter today, it is unlikely Ruskin would retain his reputation as a philanthropist.

'Iron Trees' was sparked by the Ai Weiwei exhibition of the same name.

'Parliament, Fallen' was written after Park Hill in Sheffield was renovated into private flats.

ACKNOWLEDGEMENTS

Many thanks to editors at the *Times Literary Supplement*, *Poetry London*, *PN Review*, *The Manchester Review*, *Morning Star*, in which versions of some of these poems were first published.

They also appeared in *New Poetries VII* and *Some Cannot Be Caught*.

My gratitude to Michael Schmidt, Andrew Latimer, Charlotte Rowland, Jazmine Linklater and all at Carcanet, as well as John McAuliffe and Vona Groarke.

Love also to Derm, Ciara, Aislin, Om, Trev, Amritha, Mum and Dad.